A Bear Named
Trouble

A Bear Named Trouble

Marion Dane Bauer

Clarion Books
New York

Clarion Books
a Houghton Mifflin Company imprint
215 Park Avenue South, New York, NY 10003
Copyright © 2005 by Marion Dane Bauer

The text was set in 12-point Charter ITC BT.

www.houghtonmifflinbooks.com

Printed in the U.S.A.

Library of Congress Cataloging-in-Publication Data

Bauer, Marion Dane.
A bear named Trouble / by Marion Dane Bauer.
p. cm.
Summary: In Anchorage, Alaska, two lonely youngsters make a
connection—a brown bear injured just after his mother sends him out
on his own, and a human whose father is a new keeper at the Alaska Zoo
and whose mother and sister are still in Minnesota.
ISBN 0-618-51738-3
1. Kodiak bear—Juvenile fiction. [1. Kodiak bear—Fiction.
2. Bears—Fiction. 3. Zoos—Fiction. 4. Alaska—Fiction.] I. Title.
PZ10.3.B317Be 2005
[E]—dc22
2004021259

ISBN-13: 978-0-618-51738-1
ISBN-10: 0-618-51738-3

VB   10   9   8   7   6   5   4   3   2

For all the good people at the
Alaska Zoo who rescued Trouble,
for those at the Lake Superior Zoo
who gave him a home,
and, of course,
for Trouble

Contents

1

A Bear, a Boy, a Goose

THE Alaskan brown bear wasn't born to the
name Trouble. He arrived in his six-hundred-
pound mother's den the size of a chubby chip-
munk, and for her he had no name at all. He
was merely her reason for being alive.

For the next three years of the cub's life, he
and his mother were seldom apart. He had
neither brother nor sister, so his great brown
mother was his entire world. And he must have
assumed—if bears can be said to assume—
that his life was as it would always be. He and
his mother . . . together.

Bears have no defined territory, as wolves
do and even birds. They have a range, but that
range will be overlapped by many other bears.

Consequently, they must learn a hierarchy—who has rights to the best spot along the salmon stream, who stays to feast and who moves on when the bushes hang heavy with crowberries, even who gets to nap on that smooth rock in the sun. Cubs have no status at all, but while they are with their mother, her place in the world is theirs.

During the long, long summer days in the wilderness outside Anchorage, this mother taught her son all she knew about survival. She showed him what roots and grasses and berries to eat and where to find them, the way to snatch spawning salmon from the river, how to discover the underground food caches of singing voles. She played with him, too, patient with his mock attacks, his insistent chewing on her face and ears and neck, his games of tag. And always she kept him close, calling him back if he strayed too far and nursing him many times a day. He hummed as he drew sustenance and comfort from his mother's warm body. Why should he expect this idyllic life ever to end?

Then one April day, not long after the now-adolescent bear and his mother had emerged from their third winter's den, a large male came sniffing around the open, wet area where they grazed on tufted marsh plants. In the past when another bear came near, the cub's mother had always run it off, or else she called to her son and they were the ones to move away. This time she did neither. She pretended to ignore the big fellow, but her ignoring was filled with a subtle message. "It's all right," she seemed to be saying to the intruder. "It's all right. You may stay."

The big male's being so near confused and distressed the young bear, and he moved closer to his mother's side for safety. She had up-ended a clump of sod to reveal pea-vine roots and was using her long curved claws to sift the dirt from them. The young bear bent to eat.

To the cub's surprise, when his head came near his mother's, she flattened her ears and growled, low, under her breath. He leapt away.

Bewildered, he stood for a long moment, caught between his mother's irritable warning and the intruder. Finally, he turned and sauntered a short distance from both, pretending unconcern. He dug up some wild onions and sat down to continue his breakfast.

He didn't even think about his mother again until he looked up to see her bearing down on him in a silent charge. She veered off before making contact, but the seriousness of her message couldn't have been clearer. The young bear took off at a gallop. When he reached what seemed a safe distance, he stopped to look back.

His gentle mother flattened her ears, popped her jaws, and showed her sharp yellow teeth.

The son checked the waiting male for confirmation of what had just happened. The big fellow only went on grazing, apparently unconcerned about the drama playing out before him.

The adolescent cub turned back to his

mother again and whimpered, just once. She made no response. But when he took an experimental step toward her, she lifted her snout and flattened her ears once more. No question remained.

Head hanging low, eyes dark with misery, the cub accepted his mother's sentence. He turned away.

From this day on he would be alone in the world.

*

Jonathan stood well off the zoo path, deep among the trees, so as to be away from other visitors. Here he could be alone with the pure white goose that was his favorite creature in all the zoo.

"Come, Mama Goose," he called, reaching into his pocket for the corn he always carried when he came to the zoo. "Come. Look what I have for you."

She tipped her head to one side, studying him, then suddenly flapped her great white wings and honked loudly. Jonathan jumped, just a little, and some kernels flew from his hand. As tame as she was, Mama Goose could still startle him when she did that.

When she was very young, she had been a pet. Once she'd grown past the cute, fluffy stage, her owner had decided he didn't want her after all and had donated her to the zoo. Mama Goose had a good life here. All the kids loved her. But no one, not anyone in the world, loved the pure white goose as much as Jonathan did.

"Come, Mama," he called again. And settling onto a patch of ground that wasn't too snowy, he held out a handful of corn.

Mama Goose took a cautious step toward him. She always did that, too, acted as if she had forgotten him, as if she didn't remember he was the one who came to see her every single day.

She bobbed her head up and down, took another step.

Jonathan held his breath.

And then there she was . . . not just pecking the kernels of corn out of his hand but clambering with her wide flat feet right over his legs and settling into his lap. She always gave her tail a final shake when she settled down, murmuring deep in her throat. Kind of a low chuckle.

"Hello," Jonathan whispered, running one hand down her silken neck. He took another handful of corn from his jacket pocket and held it out. Mama Goose gobbled the kernels eagerly, then tilted her head to peer with one bright eye into his face.

"Who are you?" she seemed to be saying. And, not incidentally, "Do you have any more corn?"

Jonathan laughed. "I'm Jonathan," he said. "I've told you that before. And yes . . . here's more corn."

She watched intently as his hand disappeared into his pocket and emerged again. Then she bent her elegant neck to receive the new offering.

"Just wait until Rhonda sees you,"

Jonathan said, watching her eat. "She loves birds, and she's going to love you more than all the gulls over Lake Superior. More than the bald eagles, too."

Rhonda was his little sister, but she wasn't here in Alaska with him and their father yet. When Dad moved to Anchorage to take his new job as a keeper at the Alaska Zoo, Rhonda and their mother had stayed behind in Minnesota so Mom could finish out her teaching job in Duluth. Jonathan had wanted Rhonda to come with him and Dad, but Mom had objected. "Rhonda needs me," she'd said, as though Jonathan, being all of ten years old, didn't.

In June, once school let out and their house was sold, Jonathan and Dad would fly back to Duluth and bring Mom and Rhonda and their yellow lab, Marigold, and Rhonda's beta fish, Boy Blue, to their new home in Anchorage. And then, at last, they would be a family again. But this was only April. June was a long way away.

Jonathan stroked the goose's elegant long neck again, feeling the living warmth beneath the feathers. "You'll like Rhonda, too," he told her.

She honked her agreement with that.

"I've told Rhonda I'm going to adopt you for her," he added, "so when she gets here, you'll really be hers. I'll have enough money to do it by then." He already had seventeen dollars and fifty cents toward the zoo's adoption fee of thirty dollars.

You could do that at this zoo, adopt one of the animals, and then it was as if the animal belonged to you—though whatever it was you'd adopted remained at the zoo, of course.

Imagine adopting a Siberian tiger and taking it home!

Slowly, carefully, Jonathan encircled the white goose with his arms and buried his face in the feathery softness of her breast. She tolerated his embrace briefly, then bent down to peck his ear.

"Ow!" he said, releasing her and grabbing the offended ear. "That wasn't very nice."

But nice or not, Mama Goose rose on her stubby legs, shook her feathers back into alignment, then climbed off his lap. As she waddled away, her tail feathers twitched with each step.

Jonathan smiled at the picture her rear end made—Mama Goose always made him smile—and scrambled to his feet. Though he had managed to avoid sitting in a patch of snow, his own rear was cold and more than a little damp. He wasn't done with the white goose, though, even if she was done with him. There was the game to be played still.

He closed his eyes and stood perfectly still for a long moment, breathing in the alive smell of the wet earth. When he opened them again, he was ready. It was a game he'd played with his sister since she was little. He'd pretend his way inside a bird or an animal, then he'd tell Rhonda exactly what being that animal was like.

He and Rhonda were still playing the game, even if they had to do it on the telephone now. That meant he had to store up details for the next phone call. He couldn't make the game seem real without the right details.

Jonathan squinted his eyes, studying Mama Goose, who was busy pecking at something hidden in the damp leaves.

Feathers. First there would be the feathers, soft and stiff at the same time. Feathers all over their bodies. And beaks, of course. He brought his hand up in front of his mouth, defining in the air the size and shape of a beak.

"I know," Rhonda would say, impatient for him to get on to the good part, the part where the flying began. "All birds have feathers and beaks."

"But," Jonathan would remind her for the hundredth time, "you have to be *inside* the feathers, *inside* the beak. You have to feel them."

"And inside the wings!" she would say, and without even seeing her, he would know that her cheeks were plumped out with a teasing grin.

But Jonathan refused to be hurried. He never let himself be hurried when they were playing the game, no matter how impatient Rhonda got. Waiting a little didn't hurt her. Rhonda hated waiting, but then she *was* rather spoiled. Everyone in the family admitted that Rhonda was spoiled, even Dad, who was the one who spoiled her the worst.

Next, Jonathan would remind her about Mama Goose's eyes, how she has one eye on each side of her head. "That's so she can see in every direction at once," he'd explain, "so she won't get caught by predators." But, of course, Mama Goose didn't have to worry about predators. Life in the zoo was safe.

"Our feet," Jonathan spoke out loud now, as though Rhonda were by his side and could hear, "are big and flat. You'd think a goose's feet would be cold, standing bare like that on the snow, but they aren't. It's got something to do with the veins being close together. I don't remember exactly what."

Finally, he got to the part he knew Rhonda was waiting for. He reached his arms out wide and said, "And our wings are strong. When we stretch them out, they catch the air. I can feel the way the air lifts me off the ground. I can feel the flying in my wings. Can you feel it, too?"

And without even having to close his eyes to concentrate, he heard Rhonda's answer. She looked up at him with those sky blue eyes that always captured every fragment of the light and said, "Yes, Jonnie, yes. I can feel it. Just like you. We can fly!"

2

Waiting

THE *young brown bear kept moving. Twice he circled back to check out the place where he had last seen his mother. The first time she was still there. She bared her teeth and flattened her ears again. The second time she was gone. She and the big male were both gone.*

The cub sniffed his way around the clearing. He picked up his mother's scent, but he got the intruder's, too. So . . . the two of them had gone off together. The young bear stood, gazing off after them. The trail would have been easy to follow, but bewildered as he was, he knew better than to risk an encounter with the big male.

Should he wait for his mother to return? Somehow he knew that would be futile. Once more, he turned away.

On the edge of the clearing, he paused over the yellow flower of a skunk cabbage that had melted its way through the snow. An old cinnamon-colored female bear approached with three first-year cubs tagging after. She stared at him, her head lowered, and he moved on, leaving the tiny mouthful of food untouched.

Later he stopped to scratch at a patch of bare ground, hoping to turn up more pea-vine roots. But two other three-year-olds, a brother and sister traveling together, also on their own for the first time, emerged from a clump of birch, and he loped away. They were no larger than he, but being a pair doubled their power and gave them a place in the world that he didn't have.

At every turn, another bear exerted authority over him, each of them older than he or larger or more powerful. The young bear was *growing hungry, but there was nothing to do except to keep moving.*

The smell of a ripening carcass caught his attention as he came off a small rise, running from an encounter with a larger male. Bears will kill meat when they can, but they scavenge, too. This, his nose told him, was a newborn moose calf, already dead for two or three days. A feast!

A bear's sense of smell is very sharp, and even as inexperienced as the cub was, more than the carcass should have caught his attention. But he had been running, dead out, from his last encounter, and he swerved toward the new scent without pausing to check any other smells that might have been present. He simply lunged toward the compelling odor, his mouth slavering.

What he had not reckoned with was the grieving mother, still standing watch over her dead calf. Probably he had not realized the enormous moose was there until he stopped, almost beneath her, his paws already on the ripening carcass. And before he had a chance to back off or turn or run in another direction, her front hooves flashed out, one of them catching him smartly on the jaw.

The force of the blow tumbled the young bear onto his back. But he didn't give the moose a chance to lift her great hooves for another attack. He leapt to his feet and ran once more, his roars of pain reverberating through the forest.

*

As soon as Jonathan got home from school the next day, he called Rhonda. He and Dad had an agreement that he could call Rhonda twice a week. And with the three-hour time difference between Anchorage and Minnesota, right when he got home from school was a good time. She was done with supper by then, but Mom hadn't started getting her ready for bed yet.

Rhonda had been born with a condition called spina bifida, which meant she used a wheelchair to get around. It meant, too, that even though she was six years old, Mom still did lots of stuff for her, like giving her a bath and helping her get into her pajamas.

"Guess what," he said, as soon as Rhonda was on the phone. "I dreamed about Mama Goose last night."

"You did?" She giggled. "What did she do?"

"She waddled into my room and asked me which I wanted for breakfast, pancakes or French toast."

"And what did you say?" Rhonda asked the question breathlessly, as though she couldn't wait to hear what he'd decided to have for his dream breakfast.

"Anything. I told her anything at all. As long as it isn't oatmeal!"

Rhonda laughed and laughed, her voice a chiming bell, so clear that she could have been in the next room instead of thousands of miles away. He'd have to get out a map some day and count just how many thousands.

She got the joke, of course. Mom probably would, too. When Dad was in charge of the cooking, he made oatmeal every morning of the world. Never pancakes or French toast or scrambled eggs, the way Mom did. Not even Malt-o-Meal or Cream of Wheat occasionally—always oatmeal. When Dad liked something himself, he saw no need for variation.

"Oh, Jonathan," she said when the laughter had faded away. Her voice was suddenly subdued. "When are you coming home?"

"I'm not coming home. Remember? You and Mom are going to come here."

"But you and Dad are coming to get us, aren't you?"

"Yes," Jonathan assured her as he had so many times before. "It'll just be two more months, and we'll be there."

"Two more months!" It came out as a wail, and Jonathan knew exactly how she felt. Sometimes he didn't think he could last that long, either. He didn't think he could keep taking breaths and pushing them out, over and over and over and over again, for so great a time.

It would take millions and millions of breaths, probably a trillion-trillion before he would see his mother and sister again. He should have realized when Dad had said, "We men will go on ahead," that six months would be too long. At the time, though, he'd been too pleased to be considered one of the "men" to think about the amount of time involved.

But then six months would have been too long to be away from his dad, too, so there hadn't been much of a choice.

"It'll go fast, Rhonda," he said. "Really it will."

"No, it won't," she sad. "You're lying." He could practically hear her lower lip trembling. "Two months is a long, long, *long* time." And she handed the phone to Mom without even saying goodbye.

He talked to Mom a little, but he didn't tell

her about the Mama Goose dream. Hearing her voice made him feel more homesick than ever, so he hung up as quickly as he could.

Then he walked over to the zoo. The entrance was only about half a block from his house. He poked his head through the ticket window. "Hi, Frank," he said.

"You here again?" Frank replied with mock horror. "I think you spend as much time here as your dad. We're going to have to put you to work."

"Could you?" Jonathan was filled with sudden hope. "Really?"

But Frank laughed and reached to ruffle Jonathan's hair. Jonathan could feel the heat flooding his face. Frank had been kidding. Of course! Why couldn't he ever tell when grownups were kidding?

"Here." Jonathan thrust his backpack through the window, his head lowered to hide his embarrassment. "Would you keep this for a while?" It held his homework. After he was through walking around the zoo, he'd come back and sit in the gatehouse with Frank and do his homework, waiting for his dad to get off work.

"Sure," Frank replied, taking the pack. Then he turned around, picked up a bag of freshly popped popcorn, and thrust it at Jonathan. "Would you keep this for me?"

Jonathan grinned. "Sure."

"Don't eat it now!" Frank called after Jonathan as he stepped away from the window. "I just asked you to keep it for me, not eat it."

"And don't eat my backpack," Jonathan called back cheerfully.

Still, he sighed deeply as he moved off into the zoo. Rhonda was right. Two months was a long, long, *long* time.

3

"Mama!"

THE kick the mother moose delivered while protecting her dead baby made only a glancing connection, but the blow was hard enough to break the young bear's lower jaw. It also knocked out several of his front teeth and shattered a lower canine tooth.

The cub ran and ran, moaning the whole time. He stopped occasionally to paw at the searing pain in his mouth. Then he ran some more.

He ran without considering where he was going. Sometimes, in his agony, he actually bumbled into a tangle of bushes and had to pull himself free or slopped into a marsh where the wet earth sucked at his paws. But as

soon as he broke free again, he ran some more.
He ran and bellowed. Bellowed and ran.

*

Jonathan scooped a few kernels of popcorn off the top of the bag with the tip of his tongue and stopped in front of the red fox's freestanding oval cage. The fox lay curled on a shelf high in the exhibit, peering down at him with bright button eyes.

"We had a quiz in math today," Jonathan told the fox. "It was pretty hard, but I think I got most of the answers right."

The fox blinked, yawned, tucked his long fluffy tail over his nose.

"Yeah," Jonathan agreed. "That's what I think about quizzes, too." Then, as if the fox's yawn had been catching, he yawned as well and moved on into the zoo.

The nights had been endless when they'd first come to Alaska, but now that spring was here, they were getting too short—only five or six hours of real darkness. They would get even shorter as the days moved toward summer. Dad said it would be daylight most of the time here in Anchorage by late June. Exactly the opposite of the way it had been when they arrived in January. Then the sun had stayed low on the southern horizon, peering at them through the trees for a few hours in the middle of the day. It had never really climbed into the sky, the way it was supposed to. Duluth was pretty far north, too, but not so far north that the sun couldn't make it up into the winter sky.

It wasn't just not having enough dark at night that kept him from sleeping, though. Sometimes he couldn't help lying awake, thinking about everything he had left behind.

His mother. His sister. His friends. He'd made some friends at school here, but he didn't know any of them really well yet. And none of them lived close enough to be able to get together much outside of school. He even missed the zoo back in Duluth. Lake Superior Zoo. His dad had been a keeper at

Lake Superior Zoo, and as long as Jonathan could remember, he'd loved that place. That zoo even had a waterfall and a stream running right through the middle of it. And a polar bear named Bubba who stood on his hind legs and threw a big red vinyl ball at his dad, who would toss it back.

Jonathan stopped walking. That was Mama Goose calling! He knew her imperious honk anywhere. He lifted his chin and honked back, then waited for a few beats. The entire zoo was heavily forested, the paths and the displays forming the only real break in the trees, so if she wasn't on one of the paths, it could be hard to see her. Then there she was, stiff-legging it through the trees, giving out a scolding honk with each step.

"Did you know you promised to make me breakfast this morning?" Jonathan asked her when she joined him on the path. "I asked for French toast, but you never delivered."

Mama Goose's thoughts weren't on French toast. They were on the bag of popcorn Jonathan held. She stretched her neck and danced around him, if a goose's side-to-side wobble could be considered dancing. He knelt on the path next to her and poured some of the popcorn out onto the ground. Popcorn wasn't supposed to be shared with the animals—they each had a special diet, and junk food wasn't any part of it—but Jonathan couldn't see that popcorn was so different from the corn his dad allowed.

The white goose gobbled the kernels in staccato bursts, so he poured more out, then put some into his own mouth. He let one hand rest on Mama Goose's back and sighed. Wouldn't it be wonderful if adopting an animal really did mean being allowed to take it home? Then he—and, of course, Rhonda when she came—could have Mama Goose close by all the time.

He hadn't known being in Anchorage with his dad would be so lonely. Even when Dad was home, even when they were sitting across the kitchen table from each other, eating, Jonathan often felt alone. When they were home in Duluth, he'd never noticed how little his father had to say. Somehow, with Mom and Rhonda around, the house was always cheerfully noisy. With just him and his father, the quiet seemed louder than any noise he knew how to make.

At least, he never felt lonely when he was with Mama Goose. He liked the other animals, too, but she was the best. You couldn't invite an elephant or a llama to come sit in your lap.

Maybe today, once he and Mama Goose had finished the popcorn, he would go see Ahpun and Oreo, the polar and brown bear cubs. The Alaska Zoo must be the only zoo in the world to have a polar bear and a brown bear living in the same display. Usually those kinds of bears didn't associate with each other, but these two had grown up together from the time they were orphaned as babies, and they were great friends. Dad had said they might get into trouble one day and have to be separated, but for now people came from far away to see a brown bear and a polar bear side by side.

When Rhonda got here, she could pretend to be Ahpun and he would be Oreo. Rhonda would like Ahpun best, Jonathan was certain, because the white bear swam like a seal. Rhonda would love to hear Jonathan tell about how she would feel inside Ahpun's thick white coat, how she would splash around the big pool. Round and round, upside down and sideways, even turning somersaults. Swimming the way a polar bear did was almost as good as flying.

Just thinking about Ahpun, Jonathan could feel the way the cool water flowed through his white fur. Actually, a polar bear's fur wasn't really white. His dad had told him that. It was without color, and something about the light playing on it—when his father told him, Jonathan hadn't understood exactly what it was—made it look white. But it would be white to Rhonda. And she would toss her dark curls and laugh at the freedom of skimming through the water like a fur-covered fish. Nothing, *nothing* to hold her back.

"Hi, Jon. What're you doing?"

Jonathan was so deep into his swimming reverie that he was startled at the voice. He hadn't seen his father coming. He leapt to his feet, closing the bag of popcorn as he did. "I was just going to go see Ahpun and Oreo," he said. And then, looking down at Mama Goose who was still pecking at the fluffy white kernels spread on the path, he added, "I guess I kind of spilled a little popcorn."

"Mmm," Dad said, looking down at the path and the busy goose. "Convenient to spill the popcorn when Mama Goose was near." But even as he said it, he put an arm around Jonathan's shoulders and gave him a hug, so he wasn't angry.

"Yeah," Jonathan said, giggling and looking fondly at the goose's bobbing white head. "Mighty convenient."

"Anyway, I was looking for you. We've got

a couple of orphaned moose calves that need a bottle-feeding. Like to help out?"

"Sure thing, Dad." Jonathan fell into step beside his father. "I'd like that a lot."

His dad gave his back a pat.

Jonathan skipped a couple of times to keep up with his father's long strides. Already he could feel the orphaned moose calves tugging at the bottles. Their noses would be soft and warm. Their thick pink tongues would curl around the nipples, pulling at the milk.

And before Jonathan had even arrived at the pen, he had already slipped inside one of the moose babies. He tottered on skinny, gangly legs, his big head heavy on his short neck. He reached for the bottle, and the warm milk slid down his throat. His stubby tail wagged itself into a blur.

Still, deep inside his chest something had caught into a hard knot. "Mama!" the orphaned moose calf cried, even as it took the milk in eager gulps. "Mama! Mama!"

4

The Encounter

NIGHT had fallen, but the young bear ran on without considering his destination. He had long since left behind the territory he and his mother knew, so where he went no longer mattered. All that lay before, around, behind him was new and strange.

The cub had been born and lived all his life near Anchorage, but though some bears wandered through the city itself, he and his mother had always stayed away. She had been adept at finding food for both of them. Why should she go near the strangely altered landscape of the city with its hive of humans?

As the young bear forged ahead, he hardly noticed that clipped lawns and ornamental *shrubs had begun to replace the marsh and meadow and forest he was accustomed to. He noticed little, in fact, except that his jaw hurt horribly, that he was alone, that he wanted his mother.*

He paused once to sample some grass the April melt had uncovered, but his sore mouth made chewing difficult. He moved on. He didn't stop again until he came to a strange metal object. It was saturated with a scent his mother had taught him to avoid . . . humans. But beyond the human scent was another, even more pungent. It was the totally compelling smell of rotting food.

He sniffed around the can, tipped it over with an experimental blow from one paw, and when the cover came off and rolled away, settled down to enjoy the contents. His first meal of human garbage. Delicious, delicious garbage! And much of it soft enough that he could eat it without aggravating the pain in his jaw.

He ate and ate, then moved on, looking for more.

*

Jonathan lay watching the undulating bands of light that poured through the skylight in his bedroom. Pink and blue and green flashed across the sky like a rainbow gone mad.

He thought of calling his father to come see the show, but he didn't. Dad would just point out that the northern lights came often here and that they both needed their sleep.

If his mom were here, she would watch the dancing lights with him. Jonathan could remember once when he was a very little boy and his mother plucked him, sleeping, out of his bed on a summer's night and carried him to the backyard to see a display not nearly as spectacular as this one.

He didn't remember Dad being there to watch the night sky with them, though.

Mom said that Dad was a practical man, more of a scientist than a poet. And Jonathan knew that to be true.

Mom loved poetry. She loved music and

soft trailing scarves and flowery scents. Dad came home from work smelling of the big cats, and when Jonathan had dared to say that he, too, wanted to be a zookeeper when he grew up, Dad had said, "Then you must learn to pay attention, son. You can't dream among the animals the way you do."

It didn't occur to his father that "dreaming among the animals" might be just another way of paying attention.

Jonathan closed his eyes and turned over onto his side. Dad was right about one thing. He did need to get some sleep. Another quiz tomorrow. Social studies this time. Why didn't anyone ever ask him what it felt like to be a polar bear . . . or a moose calf . . . or a white goose? Now *that* would be something worth taking a quiz about!

Jonathan was just drifting toward sleep when a sound brought him awake again. A thud . . . like something falling. Like *someone* falling. It seemed to come from the deck just below his window.

He jumped out of bed, taking a tangle of covers with him. He kicked the blankets aside and peered out the window. Despite a light layer of new snow on the deck, it was too dark down there to see anything. He scrabbled under the bed for his slippers. He couldn't go outside without something on his feet. He found one moccasin-style slipper and one sneaker and pulled them on. The sneaker was for the wrong foot, but he didn't care.

He hurried down the stairs on tiptoe. At the sliding deck door he stopped and peered out. The house was surrounded by enormous fir trees, so even though the sky still flashed brightly, the shadows of the tall trees fell across the deck, obscuring everything.

Jonathan flipped on the light switch. No light. Of course. That was his fault. Before supper, Dad had asked him to replace the bulb on the deck. He had said he would—and he'd meant to do it, really—but then he'd forgotten.

Another sound. Almost a moan. Someone in pain?

Dad? Had his father gone outside and fallen down because the bulb hadn't been replaced? Maybe he had come out to see the northern lights blazing across the sky after all.

Quickly, silently, Jonathan slid the glass door open and stepped out onto the deck. The cold night air slapped him in the face. It would be a long time before it would be warm here, longer even than it took to warm up in Duluth. Snow crunched lightly under his feet.

He could see nothing. "Dad?" he called in a voice that surprised even him with its tremor. "Are you out here?"

No answer. Only that noise again, a little louder this time. Jonathan took another step.

And then he saw. Not his father. A brownie! It wasn't full grown, but plenty big enough. And close enough, too! The shadowy hulk rose not six feet from the spot where

Jonathan stood. Jonathan could make out the hump of muscle between the shoulders and the profile of the slightly scooped face that distinguishes brown bears from black.

The other way people said you could tell the difference between the two was that if you climbed a tree, a black bear would climb up after you and eat you. A brown bear would stay on the ground and shake you out of the tree and *then* eat you. Jonathan wished he could manage not to remember things like that.

The bear stood so close that Jonathan could smell the rotting food on the brownie's breath and some other, darker smell that must be the bear himself. If the creature had wanted to, he could have reached out and knocked Jonathan down with one of those huge paws. But he didn't seem to want to. In fact, as surprised as Jonathan was to be standing there on his own deck staring into the eyes of a bear, the bear seemed equally surprised to be confronted by a boy.

And then, with a kind of strangled moan, a sound similar to the one Rhonda made when Mom was brushing tangles out of her long hair and she was trying really hard not to cry, the brownie bounded past Jonathan, down the snowy steps and was gone.

Jonathan stood rooted for a long moment listening to the pounding of his own heart.

5

Hunger

THE bear kept moving, steadily, stopping now and then to nose at a possible source of food. Everything around him was totally unfamiliar, but the smell of food seemed to permeate the air. Along with the smell of humans.

Still . . . the human he had just encountered hadn't hurt him. And here, surrounded by their presence, and their smell, other bears didn't appear at every turn to run him off.

He came across a bird feeder and rose on his hind legs to take it delicately between his paws. His long tongue took up the task of drawing every last seed into his mouth.

Maybe this strange human place would be his new range.

If only he weren't so lonely.

*

"Jonathan!"

The name drifted up from the bottom of the stairwell, and Jonathan came awake suddenly. Not Jon. Not Jonnie. *Jonathan.* He must be in trouble. He sat up, instantly awake. "Yeah?" he called back.

"Would you come down here, please?"

What had he done now? He couldn't figure. He'd washed the dishes last night, hadn't he? The few dishes left over from the boxed macaroni and cheese Dad had fixed. Mom made mac and cheese from scratch, a whole different dish. Hers was creamy and sharp with good cheddar. The stuff Dad had made—

"Jonathan? Are you coming?"

"Yes, Dad." He put his feet on the cold floor, dropping his head between his knees to look under his bed for his slippers. One was out of reach in the far corner. The other was close at hand, as was one black, high-topped sneaker. They would do.

It was the pulling on of the mismatched footwear that brought the memory back. The bear! He had met a brownie on the deck last night. Wait until Dad heard!

Jonathan hurried down the stairs.

He didn't have a chance to tell his wonderful news, though. When he arrived, his father was already talking. "Look at that, would you?" he was saying. And then, "I'd like an explanation." He pointed toward the deck.

Jonathan looked. There it was, imprinted in the thin layer of new snow on the deck, a complete record of last night's adventure. Bear tracks. The tracks of a brown bear for sure, because black bear tracks are broken. The pads on black bears' feet aren't solid. Brownie tracks look more like a whole human footprint. A very large human footprint.

And there were his own footprints, too. The one smooth—that was his moccasin—the other crisscrossed with diamonds, his wrong-footed sneaker. The two sets of tracks faced one another. Close. Very close. Looking at them, Jonathan could almost smell the brownie again. He had never smelled a brownie before.

Dad looked down at Jonathan's oddly clad feet, then up at his face. "Jonathan?" he said again. The name formed a question, a serious one.

"I heard a noise," Jonathan said, the words coming out in a rush. "I came downstairs because I heard a noise. I thought maybe it was you. That you'd gone on the deck and had fallen down or something. I didn't know it was a brownie until I went outside. And then I—" The flow of words stopped as abruptly as it had begun, and Jonathan waited. Was his father going to be angry?

But Dad said only, "And then you practically bumped into it from the looks of things."

"Yeah," Jonathan admitted with a shrug. "I think we were both surprised."

"I'll bet." His father was stroking the dark

stubble on his chin in that way he had when he was amused and trying not to show it. But then his eyebrows pulled together and the amusement—if that is what it had been—passed. "You know," he said, "that brown bears are dangerous. It's not like the black bears that we used to see sometimes in Duluth."

Jonathan nodded. He had heard the lecture. Dad had given it before they moved here and at least once every couple of weeks since they'd arrived. But then his father used to warn him about the Minnesota black bears when they lived in Duluth, too. Once, when he was in kindergarten, he had been walking to school along a hedge and when he came to the end of the hedge, he found himself nose to nose with a black bear that had been walking along on the other side. When he'd gone home to tell the story, his father had given him a stern warning about that bear—as though he'd invited the creature to walk to school with him.

"The brownie didn't do anything, Dad. He just looked at me. And I looked at him. Then he ran off."

"You were lucky."

Jonathan nodded. Of course. He knew he'd been lucky. His pounding heart had told him that last night.

"Remember, Jon. Brownies aren't teddy bears. They're wild animals. And very dangerous. Next time don't be so quick to go waltzing out onto the deck. If you hear a noise outside, come wake me up instead."

Jonathan nodded. "Sure, Dad," he said. He knew perfectly well that his father was right, though he couldn't help wondering, just a bit, what Dad would have said last night if he had awakened him. Perhaps: *There's nothing out there . . . nothing. Go back to bed.*

In any case, his answer satisfied his father. Dad nodded and headed back upstairs to take a shower.

Alone just inside the sliding deck door,

Jonathan didn't move. He stood still, one hand on the cool glass, feeling a shaggy brown coat growing, feeling the way it protected him from heat and cold alike. He could feel his great muscles rippling beneath all that fur, too.

And he could feel his hunger.

His hunger was huge, and mere food didn't begin to satisfy it.

6

Break-in

THE young bear had slept through the day in a clump of trees. Now it was evening again, and he woke to search for food once more. In the wild, he usually slept at night, but in this place, with humans everywhere, he had quickly adapted his habits to hiding himself away and sleeping in the daytime.

His jaw still ached miserably. Only the softest food would do. But there seemed to be plenty of that here.

He had visited a couple more garbage cans and several bird feeders when he came to a tall fence. He turned and began to follow along its length. From beyond the fence more good smells came. Food. All kinds of food. But even more important, now that his stomach no longer ached with hunger, he could make out the distinct smell of another bear.

Not his mother. He knew his mother's smell the way he knew his own. But one of his own kind, nonetheless. A male.

He should have been afraid. He should have known to go far away, but he was drawn toward the scent as if he were being pulled by a rope. He was so lonely.

At the bottom of a small ravine a creek passed beneath the fence. The young bear began digging. When he had hollowed out enough space to squeeze through, he did. And he did the same thing at the next fence he encountered. Then he set off at a lope to find the bear.

A white goose honked at him, her voice strident, commanding, but the young bear paid no attention. He was on a mission.

*

Jonathan poked his head through the ticket window.

"Guess what!" Frank was grinning. "We had a break-in last night."

Jonathan gasped. "A break-in?"

"Yeah. A wild brownie came to visit Jake. This morning you could see his footprints in the snow all up and down by Jake's pen. Apparently, the two of them walked up and down all night, talking to each other."

Jake was one of the resident brown bears, a large Kodiak. He had lived with his sister from the time both were cubs, but his sister had died the year before. Usually an older male would have no interest in a younger one . . . except to prove his dominance. But maybe Jake didn't like living by himself.

"Have they caught him? The wild one, I mean." Waiting for an answer, Jonathan held his breath. Why was it that he knew so emphatically that he didn't want the brownie caught?

"Nah. This morning your dad found him asleep between the two fences, right by the stream where he'd dug in. But he scooted out again before anyone could figure out what to do about him."

Jonathan breathed a sigh of relief. Then his bear was all right.

It *must* be his bear, the one that had visited his deck the night before last. He didn't know why he knew that, but he did.

Jonathan left his backpack, accepted the usual bag of popcorn, and headed toward the enclosure that held Jake. Just wait until the next day at school when he told his friends! A brownie breaking *into* the zoo!

Had such a thing ever happened before in all the history of zoos?

But then maybe he wouldn't tell them. He didn't know why, exactly, but he kept his friends separate from his life at the zoo. It had been that way in Minnesota, too. The zoo, his dreams about being inside the animals . . . all that belonged to him and Rhonda, no one else. Not even Mom knew about the game they played.

A raucous honking stopped him in his

tracks. "Hello, Mama," he said. "Did you meet the visitor last night?"

She honked again, sounding indignant.

Jonathan laughed. "If you did, I guess you didn't like him all that much."

He poured some popcorn out onto the ground and watched Mama Goose go to work on it.

"He's *my* bear, you know," Jonathan confided. "He came to visit *me* first."

Mama Goose ignored him, intent on the popcorn. When she had gobbled the last kernel, she pecked at his shoe.

"That's all you think about, isn't it?" Jonathan scolded. "Something to fill your belly." But even as he said it, he ran a hand down the goose's supple neck, feeling the lively movement beneath the downy feathers. "Well . . . here. I'm not all that hungry anyway." He poured the rest of the popcorn onto the ground, then crumpled the bag and stuck it in his jacket pocket. "Enjoy," he told the white goose, though she was clearly already doing just that.

As he moved toward Jake's pen, he felt his body fold down until, in his mind, he was walking on all fours, his feet flat to the ground. His four sturdy legs moved in a steady rhythm; his heavy coat rippled with each loping step. He was a wild brownie, and he was hungry, and he had just broken into the zoo.

Lumbering along, he could feel the bear's longing. Not just for food. Nor for a caged companion he couldn't even reach. For something more than that, Jonathan was certain. But what?

7

"No!"

JONATHAN crept down the stairs in the dark. The occasional low snorts coming from his father's bedroom told him Dad was asleep, but he still didn't want to turn on a light. You never knew when he might awaken and start to ask questions.

In the kitchen Jonathan found the loaf of bread Dad had bought just yesterday. He started to open it to take out a few slices, but then he closed it up and picked up the entire loaf instead. A few slices of bread would hardly make a snack for a bear. Jonathan wanted the brownie to stay around awhile so he could watch him.

Outside, he looked both ways, half expecting the bear to be out there already, watching from the shadow of the trees that loomed at the edge of his yard. Then he laid the loaf of bread on the deck, still in its plastic wrapper. A thin wrapper like that would be no hindrance to a bear. And if no bear came, he could wipe off the plastic, bring the bread back to the kitchen, and Dad would never need to know that the bread for his lunch sandwiches had spent the night out in the cold.

But if the bear did come . . .

Jonathan's heart raced at the thought.

Another thought followed in rapid succession. What was he going to say in the morning when his father couldn't find the bread? That was going to be one interesting conversation. Jonathan could hardly admit that he'd put the bread out hoping the bear would come by again. Luring wild animals with food was an even worse offense than disrupting the carefully planned diets of the ones being held in the zoo.

Would Dad believe him if he said he'd gotten hungry during the night and eaten the whole loaf himself?

Jonathan shrugged, stepped back inside, and carefully, quietly slid the glass door shut. The morning would have to take care of itself. Right now he wanted to see the brownie again.

He turned on the deck light—he'd put in a fresh bulb before dinner—pulled an armchair close to the deck door, and curled up in it to wait.

"Come on, bear," he whispered. "Come on!"

*

Again the young bear had spent the day sleeping, hidden in a thick clump of trees. The land was heavily treed, both inside and outside the zoo, so it was easy for him to find safe and private places to sleep. But now night had fallen, and he prowled once more.

This night was less successful than the one before. He couldn't find any garbage cans this

*time. He located another bird feeder and
smashed it into splinters trying to get the re-
maining few seeds out. And then, whether by accident or intent, he ended up at the deck where
he had met the young human before, though
he had found no food there the first time.*

*This time he was lucky. A full loaf of bread
lay waiting, and he gobbled it, plastic wrapper
and all.*

*His jaw still ached, and the teeth didn't
mesh on the side where the moose had kicked
him, but the bread was soft and went down in
quick gulps.*

*

A shiver passed down Jonathan's spine as
he watched the bread disappear. He had
thought a whole loaf was a lot. It would
have been a lot for him and his father. They
would have taken the entire week to eat it
all. But he could see now that a loaf would
barely dent the hunger of so large an animal.

The bear had swallowed the last mouthful and now licked the deck for crumbs. It was snowing again, fat, round flakes that swirled lazily in the light.

Sitting until the bear showed up had been hard. In fact, Jonathan had been pretty much asleep when the brownie finally appeared. He might have come and gone without being seen if Jonathan hadn't been pulled awake by the click of his long claws against the wooden deck floor. When the sound awakened him, he'd leapt to the sliding door for a better look.

"Where are you going next, bear?" he asked now, tapping lightly on the glass.

As though he had known all along that the human who had put out the bread was close, the brownie lifted his head and looked straight into Jonathan's eyes. Jonathan found himself stepping back, his skin suddenly prickling with cold, his mouth dry. Nonetheless, when the big animal turned and shuffled off the deck, Jonathan grabbed his coat and, being careful not to make a sound that might carry upstairs to his father, slipped through the sliding door.

The bear seemed to know exactly where he was going, and Jonathan followed, keeping what seemed a safe distance behind. In just a few minutes they were at the fence surrounding the zoo. The bear went immediately to the place where he had dug the night before, at the point the stream flowed under the fence. Jonathan knew, though, that Charlie, one of the maintenance men, had filled the spot in. Jonathan had watched him do it. Charlie must have done something to harden the fill, too, because the bear tried digging in the same spot once, then moved off to one side and began digging for real.

Jonathan kept a tree between himself and the brownie, but stayed close enough to see what he was doing. After the young bear had scooted under the fence on his belly, Jonathan approached the fence cautiously. He waited for the bear to dig under the second fence, too, then got down low and scooted after him. His jacket and his pajama bottoms were getting muddy, but he couldn't worry about that.

By the time Jonathan emerged from beneath the second chain-link fence, Mama Goose was making her usual racket. Obviously, she considered herself the guardian of the zoo and didn't approve of intruders.

"Honk . . . honk . . . honk!" she scolded.

For an instant, Jonathan let himself slip inside the goose, feeling her loud indignation. He smiled. She was one brave bird to stand against a brownie!

The bear had moved on ahead, covering the ground faster than Jonathan could. He was heading for Jake's holding area again. But apparently the ruckus Mama Goose was making disturbed him. He paused and turned back. Jonathan caught up with him just in time to see the bear lift a great paw and swing at the noisy goose.

The blow lifted Mama Goose from the

ground in a sudden white arc. She landed in a rumpled heap.

"No!" Jonathan cried. His voice was the only sound on the night air.

The bear paused, peering down at the fallen goose, as though he didn't understand what had caused her noise to stop so abruptly. He poked his nose beneath her, lifting her slightly from the ground, then letting her drop again. Then he turned away and lumbered toward Jake's cage, clearly unconcerned with the murder he had just committed.

For the space of several heartbeats, Jonathan couldn't move. He couldn't lift a hand or a foot or even, it seemed, blink his eyes. Then he ran and dropped to his knees before Mama Goose. The white feathers were soft, soft in his hands. He picked up the rag-doll body and held it tightly against his chest, the head dangling awkwardly over his arm.

She was so heavy, heavier than she had

ever seemed when she had climbed into his lap, and utterly still.

Beneath the soft feathers Jonathan could feel the life seeping out of Mama Goose, rushing away . . . rushing . . . gone.

8

Trouble

"HE killed her! He killed her! He killed Mama Goose! She's dead!"

The words erupted from Jonathan in a shout. He filled the night air with his outrage the whole way home. He shouted and sobbed and ran, clutching the white goose close to his chest. He kept picking up her head, trying to keep it from dangling so pitifully, but each time the silence of the feathery head, the unnatural weight of it in his hand, made his fingers go slack, and he let it fall again. He tumbled through the sliding deck door and hurtled up the stairs to his dad's bedroom.

Halfway between the bedroom door and

the bed, Jonathan stopped and shouted it all again. "He killed her! He killed Mama! She's dead!"

His father lurched upright, rising so fast that Jonathan stepped back a couple of steps. But he didn't stop crying out. "She's dead! She's dead!"

"What!" His dad's brown hair stood in spikes all over his head, and his eyes were open so wide that they were rimmed all the way around with white. "Jonnie! What is it? What's wrong?"

"That bear!" Jonathan was sobbing now. He leaned back against the wall next to the door. "That bear. He killed Mama Goose."

"Oh," his father said. "Oh! Mama *Goose*." And his spine suddenly slumped. "I thought . . . I thought . . ." He didn't say what he had thought, just reached out as if to capture Jonathan's hand, but Jonathan was too far away for him to reach. "Come here, son." He beckoned. "You were having a dream. Only a dream. That bear isn't going to hurt any—"

But when Jonathan approached, a thin beam of moonlight fell across the goose clutched to his chest, and Dad's gaze fastened there. "What?" He reached out and touched Mama Goose's dangling head, just lightly. Then he reached beyond the goose to the front of Jonathan's muddy jacket. "Where—where have you been?"

He was fully awake now. He even ran a hand through his standing-up hair to smooth it down.

"That bear." Jonathan gasped for breath. "The brownie that broke into the zoo. He did it again. And this time he killed her."

Dad had his feet on the floor now. His bare feet looked pale and somehow very naked. He reached for a robe and slippers. "You were there?" His voice was stern, but when he lifted Mama Goose from Jonathan's grasp and put a hand on his shoulder to lead him back downstairs, his touch was gentle.

First Dad opened the sliding door and laid the dead goose on the snowy deck, then he closed the door again and, brushing his hands on his robe as if something about death might cling to them, pulled the drapes closed.

Jonathan let his knees give way and sank to the couch.

"Now tell me," his father said, coming to stand in front of him. "All of it."

Jonathan told "all of it" between hiccupping sobs. About luring the bear to the deck by putting out the loaf of bread. About following him into the zoo, under the fence. About seeing him strike Mama Goose.

As Jonathan spoke, his father's lips grew thinner, tighter, but when he finally fell silent, Dad said only, "I'm sorry. I'm sorry it happened, son. And I'm especially sorry you were there to see it." And without another word, he headed back toward the stairs.

"Where are you going?" Jonathan asked, suddenly wanting, more than anything else, for his father not to leave.

"I have to go over there," Dad said, stopping at the foot of the stairs, "to see what other mischief that bear might be getting into. I need to call the curator, too. And I'll take Mama Goose back where she belongs."

"May I come?" Jonathan asked, but he knew the answer.

"Of course not." For the first time, his father sounded impatient, as he surely was. He hadn't even mentioned yet all the rules Jonathan had broken tonight, but he would get to them later. Jonathan was sure of that.

He came back to stand in front of Jonathan again. "You stay here and see if you can get the mud off your jacket. You'll need it for school tomorrow." He paused, studying Jonathan closely, as though he might be wondering if he'd made a mistake bringing him here to Anchorage. But then he continued in his ordinary father-in-charge voice. "And clean yourself up, too. Then go to bed. Get right into bed and don't get out of it again until morning. Do you understand? I'll be back as soon as I can."

"Why can't I . . ." Jonathan started to say,

but his father whirled to face him, his eyes flashing, and Jonathan shrank back into the couch cushions. "Yes, sir," he said. He didn't know where that had come from . . . *sir*. He had never called his father *sir* in his life. But then he had never seen his father this angry before, either. "I promise."

"You'd better," his father said, his voice low. Then he added, "We're going to have plenty to talk about when I get back." He hurried up the stairs.

Jonathan looked down at his muddy jacket. Was Mama Goose muddy, too? He'd had to crawl out beneath the fence as he'd gone in, holding her the whole time. There was no other way out without a key. Had he gotten Mama Goose muddy? Somehow—he didn't know why—the idea of her pure white feathers being caked with mud seemed the final insult. He'd never seen her when her feathers weren't clean.

But then being dead changed everything, didn't it? Everything in the world.

*

The young bear had walked up and down the fence enclosing the older male but could find no way to get closer. Jake had paced on his side, too, sniffed through the fence, then paced some more.

It was Jake who gave up first, turning back into his enclosure to sleep. And the young bear, abandoned once more, retraced his steps through the zoo. He found bits of food here and there, stopped to sniff the place where the white goose had lain, then bellied under the inner fence around the perimeter and decided to go no farther. He took a long drink from the creek before he curled up in a snowy depression in the ground between the two fences and dozed.

He didn't come awake until he heard the voices of the humans, moving closer. He listened, his head raised, his ears pivoting to catch every nuance of sound. Finally, he rose slowly, walked over to the hole beneath the outer fence he had dug earlier, and shimmied out the way he had come in.

The searching men again found footprints in the fresh snow up and down in front of Jake's pen. They found a few scattered white feathers. And they found a new hole dug under both of the perimeter fences.

"I think," Jonathan's father said, "we should name this bear Trouble. That's certainly what he's gotten into lately."

9

Take Care of Trouble

"TROUBLE? You named that bear Trouble?" Disobeying one more order, Jonathan had slept on the living room couch while his father was gone, and he sat up now, bleary eyed but nonetheless awake.

"Yes," his father replied. "Do you have a better suggestion?"

Jonathan didn't even have to pause to consider. "Killer," he said. "You should call him Killer. That's what he is."

His father sighed. "He's a bear, Jonnie. He did what bears do. It's what I've been trying to tell you."

Jonathan shook his head, trying to clear away the image of Mama Goose, dead and limp . . . and so soft in his arms. He said, "I thought bears killed to eat. He didn't want her for food. He barely stopped long enough to smell her. Just knocked her dead and went on his way."

Dad sighed again. Jonathan could tell he was growing exasperated. "What do you want me to do?"

"Capture him! Take him away! Take him so far away he can never come back again," Jonathan cried. "He's dangerous. You can't let him stay here."

His father looked surprised. He also looked enormously tired. "Well, we're going to have to catch him first, before we can do anything. But zoos aren't in the business of transporting animals. Besides . . ." But he didn't say any more.

"He's a murderer," Jonathan said. "He's got to be taken away!"

His father shook his head. "I think we're mighty lucky that Mama Goose was the only fatality last night. What were you thinking of, anyway, luring a bear to our deck with food and then following him through the night?"

"I stayed back. Out of the way."

Dad snorted, a tiny puff of exasperated breath. "Do you have any idea how fast that brownie could run if he decided he didn't want you following him and came at you?"

"Thirty miles an hour, I guess." Jonathan had read it somewhere. "Maybe more."

"Yes," his dad replied. "And do you think you can run thirty miles an hour, maybe more?"

Jonathan shrugged. When his father drew his eyebrows together in irritation, he said, "No. I don't suppose I can."

"Jonnie." His dad came over and sat down on the couch beside him. "How many times do I have to tell you? Bears are wild animals. Even the ones in the zoo like Jake. He's been around humans since he was a baby. And do you know how far I'd trust him if I had to go into his cage when he was in there?"

Jonathan started to shrug again, to show that he didn't know, didn't care, but then he stopped. There was no point in annoying his father further. "Not very far," he said.

"You're darned right. No farther than I could throw the big brute if he came at me."

Jonathan nodded. "Anyway," he said, trying to sound reasonable so his father would listen, "Mama Goose wasn't doing anything to him. Just making a lot of noise, the way she always does. All he wanted was to shut her up. And he . . . he . . ." Jonathan swung one hand as though it were a big paw and found that he could speak no further. His throat had closed.

"I know, son. I know." His dad put an arm around his shoulders. "And I'm sorry it happened. I know you really liked that old goose."

Really liked! That didn't begin to describe it. But all Jonathan said was, "Rhonda loved her, too. I'd told Rhonda all about her, and you know how she loves birds. She thought

Mama Goose was even better than the sea-gulls we used to watch over Lake Superior."

"Yes," Dad agreed, "I'm sure Rhonda loved her, too, just hearing about her from you. But there you are. She's gone now. Actually, I think your *she* may have been a *he*."

"Mama Goose? A boy?" Jonathan almost laughed, but then he began to cry instead, big wracking sobs that seemed to rise from the soles of his feet. He didn't think he'd tell Rhonda that. Too confusing. But he didn't know what he'd say to her on the phone now. Mama Goose was mostly what they'd talked about since he'd gotten here.

His father said nothing more. He just pulled Jonathan closer. "I've got an idea," he said, stroking the hair back from Jonathan's face. "I think this would be a good day for you to stay home from school. I'll bet even your mama would agree if she were here to see you now."

Jonathan sniffed, wiped his nose on his pajama sleeve, and half laughed. Being a teacher, his mother found very few excuses good enough for staying home from school. Fever, vomiting, or something major broken. That was about it.

Would she understand about Mama Goose?

"What . . . what'll I do all day?" he asked, though already he knew one thing he wanted to do if he was left alone in the house.

"Oh, I don't know," his dad replied. "Read. Watch a bit of television. Maybe write a letter to one of your friends. How does that sound?"

"Okay," Jonathan said. And then, in case he hadn't sounded enthusiastic enough and his dad might change his mind, he sat up straight and said, "Good!"

Dad stood and pulled Jonathan gently to his feet. "Why don't you start with a shower? Maybe followed by another nap. You must have missed a lot of sleep last night."

Jonathan nodded and headed for the stairs. He'd start with a shower. No problem.

But he wasn't the least bit interested in a nap. In fact, a plan was developing for when his dad left to go back to the zoo. He was going to call one of the local TV stations and tell them all about Trouble. If they reported that a wild bear had killed Mama Goose, someone would have to do something about him for sure.

Jonathan stood in the shower a long time, letting the hot water slam into his head, his face. He stayed so long, in fact, and dressed so slowly that Dad had already eaten his oatmeal and gone back to the zoo by the time he came downstairs. So he fixed himself some Cheerios, even put his muddy jacket and the pajamas he'd been wearing into the washing machine. Then he got the phone book out to look up the number.

The ring at the other end seemed to buzz inside his head.

He waited.

"KTUU, Channel Two," said a woman's voice.

"Um . . ." Jonathan's mouth went suddenly dry. He'd never talked to anyone from a television station before. "Um," he said again. Why hadn't he figured out what he was going to say before he'd dialed?

"KTUU, Channel Two," the woman said again, a little impatiently this time.

And so he blurted it out, the thing they needed to know. "I've got some news for you. It's something you're going to want to do a story on. There's a killer on the loose in Anchorage."

*

For a while, Trouble kept moving away from the zoo. The trees in this residential area of the city were heavy. Keeping hidden from the humans who were beginning to emerge was not difficult. And if there were other bears anywhere around to challenge him for the bits of food he occasionally found, he didn't encounter them.

After a time, though, he turned and retraced his steps until he was back at the outer zoo fence again. He prowled along it for a short distance until he came to a dip in the ground beneath some fir trees. He curled up in the inviting gloom of the trees, tucking his aching muzzle beneath a paw, and waited. Just waited.

When it grew dark, he would go in search of food again, and maybe, at last, he would find a way to reach the bear behind the fence.

10

"Good!"

"AND not only did the wild bear, named Trouble by one of the keepers, break into the zoo. While he was inside, he killed Mama Goose, a snow white goose that was a favorite of visiting children."

The newscaster reporting the story stood in front of Jake's enclosure, but Jake, apparently shunning publicity, was nowhere in sight. Jonathan sat on the couch next to his father, watching the news program, but out of the corner of his eye he was really watching his father.

Dad shook his head. "I sure would like to know who told them," he said. "When they showed up at the zoo, there wasn't much we could do but let them in. They already knew the whole story."

Jonathan felt a flicker of guilt, but only a flicker. Some things just had to be told. His father should understand that. He'd had a hard time, at first, convincing the man the receptionist had turned him over to—not the reporter giving the story now, but some kind of editor—that his story was real. Only when Jonathan had finally told him that his dad was one of the keepers at the zoo had the man started to listen.

Now the camera was showing footprints in the layer of fresh snow along Jake's fence. There were bear footprints on both sides of the fence. But Jonathan was through listening. He'd gotten what he wanted. The world knew that a wild bear had broken into the zoo and killed Mama Goose, "a favorite of visiting children."

The phone rang. Dad got up wearily to answer it.

Jonathan leaned back into the couch,

paying no attention to the conversation. It wouldn't be Mom. She and Dad had talked a long time last night, so she probably wouldn't call tonight.

What would he tell Rhonda when he talked to her next time? Some of the stories he'd told her about Mama Goose might have been a bit exaggerated, he'd admit that—like when he'd told her that Mama Goose came running to meet him every time he came to the zoo. But he'd told her true things, too. Like about the way Mama Goose would honk back when you honked at her. Rhonda was really excited about meeting her very own goose.

"Well, that's it," Dad said, hanging up the phone and returning to the couch.

"What's it?" Jonathan asked.

"That was Pat Rawlings, the curator. Somebody called him from Fish and Game."

"Yeah?" Jonathan said, not particularly interested. The news program had moved on, but they were still talking about bears. This segment was about how important it was for homeowners not to attract bears by leaving garbage cans out or having bird feeders that could be reached. *Or loaves of bread on their decks,* Jonathan added mentally.

The newscaster was saying that about two hundred and fifty black bears lived in the Anchorage area and about sixty brown bears, too. "When they lose their fear of humans because they associate us with food, they can become extremely dangerous."

"One of the rangers heard the news report about Trouble," Dad said.

Jonathan sat up straighter, turning his full attention to his father for the first time.

"Next time that bear breaks into the zoo, they want to be informed."

"Why?" Jonathan asked, although he knew. Of course, he knew.

"When Trouble leaves the zoo, they're going to take care of him."

"'Take care' of Trouble," Jonathan repeated slowly. "What does that mean?"

"They're going to put him down." His

father said it in a flat voice, not looking in Jonathan's direction.

Put him down. For an instant Jonathan felt as though he had been kicked in the gut. Put Trouble down. Off him. *Kill* him. So Trouble would end up as dead, as limp, as useless as Mama Goose!

"Why can't they just take him away, some place so far that he can never come back here?"

"Because they have a firm policy," his father said. "Once a bear loses his fear of people, he'll get into trouble wherever he goes. He's too dangerous to be allowed to live anywhere. Bears like that have to be destroyed."

Jonathan's head spun. For a moment, he thought he might be ill. But then he drew himself up and took a deep, wavering breath. "Good!" he said. He said it as though he meant it, too.

After all, Trouble would only be getting what he deserved. Wouldn't he?

*

Trouble stood outside the fence to Jake's enclosure and moaned softly. The older bear, apparently having tired of the nightly encounters, didn't respond. He didn't even emerge from his den. Trouble would have dug under this fence, too, but unlike the perimeter fences that were meant only to keep humans out, the fences enclosing the animals were set in concrete.

Finally, the young bear sat, then after another long period of waiting, curled into a ball right there, tight against the fence that kept him separated from Jake. He was miserable. He wasn't finding enough food, and his stomach roared at him. His broken jaw had never quit pounding from the instant the moose had kicked him.

But most fiercely of all, he still missed his mother. More than he wanted the pain to go away, more than he wanted food to fill his empty belly, he was still a very young bear, and he wanted his mother.

11

Trouble for Trouble

JONATHAN'S house was so close to the zoo that he could see the parking lot and the entrance gate from the corner where he waited for the school bus. He watched both now.

He had told his father that he needed another day away from school. He'd reminded him, after all, that he was still terribly upset about seeing Mama Goose murdered.

His father had said, "Um-hmm," in that way he always did when he wasn't really listening, when he didn't think what Jonathan was saying was worth listening to, and then handed him his lunch bag. So now Jonathan was standing at the corner, waiting for the bus.

The hour was too early for the zoo to be open, but nonetheless a truck pulled up to the gate. On the side was written ALASKA DEPARTMENT OF FISH AND GAME. The man who emerged held a rifle in one hand.

Jonathan couldn't tell whether it was a real gun or one that shot tranquilizer darts, but he supposed it didn't matter whether they shot Trouble outright or tranquilized him now, then killed him later. Either way the dumb bear was going to be dead. Good and dead.

But was dead ever good? Jonathan didn't know. To keep himself from asking more stupid questions he turned his thoughts to Mama Goose again . . . limp and silent, a pile of white feathers. Certainly there was nothing good about her being dead.

Jonathan walked a dozen steps away from the corner, then returned to his former spot, right where the bus always stopped.

It was what Trouble deserved, wasn't it? For someone to kill him the way he had killed

Rhonda's goose. Not an instant's thought, just *bam!* and the bear would be gone. After all, Trouble had no business killing Mama Goose just because she was making a little noise. She/he. Nothing made sense any more.

And now the whole world knew about Trouble's crime, and justice would be served . . . exactly the way they always said in crime shows.

Another vehicle pulled up in front of the zoo, a white van with KTUU written on the side. A man got out and stood talking to the Fish and Game guy. After a while, he went back to the van and returned carrying a TV camera.

So, not only were they going to kill Trouble, they were going to film the event so everyone in town could watch it while they ate their supper tonight.

Jonathan's stomach did a slow flip-flop.

Would there be blood? Would there be lots of blood?

It wouldn't matter if there was, would it? Seeing Trouble die on TV would be like watching a bad guy get blasted away in a crime show. Nothing more.

He'd seen lots of blood on TV, lots of creatures and even people dying. But you always knew the blood you saw there—however red it might be—was really fake. The blood, the limp body, all of it was fake.

Trouble's death would be different, though. It would be real. Because Trouble was real. At least he would be for a little while longer.

Would he still be real after the Fish and Game guy finished with him?

Jonathan turned away from the men in the parking lot and looked down the road instead. Still no sign of the school bus.

Why had his father given that stupid bear a name? Everything would be easier if Trouble were still just "the bear." There were lots of bears out there. Lots and lots. But the moment you gave one a name—even a not-very-friendly name like Trouble—he became the only one. There was no other "Trouble." So did that mean that what happened to Trouble mattered?

Jonathan took a deep breath, and just as he let it out he saw the top of a yellow bus rising out of a dip in the road. He tightened his hold on his lunch bag and hunched deeper into his jacket.

The bus rumbled to a stop and the door *shush*ed open. Jonathan stared at the open door and at the metal steps climbing up into the bus, then he stepped back.

"Hi, Jonnie," Dorothy, the driver, said. "Missed you yesterday. Were you sick?"

"Uh," he said. "Uh. Yeah . . . kind of." But he didn't move from where he stood, his shoes rooted to the half-frozen ground. A mew gull flew over, making its familiar sound that seemed almost like crying.

Dorothy said nothing more. She just waited, her round face smiling, her arms crossed, leaning on the steering wheel as though she had all the time in the world.

Jonathan took another step back. "You know," he said, holding his free hand in front of his face as though to shield himself from the force of Dorothy's smile, "I guess I'd better go back home. I think I forgot something."

He expected the bus driver to argue, to tell him, as his mother would have, to get on the bus and quit being silly. If she had done that, no doubt he would have obeyed. He was not accustomed to ignoring orders from adults. But, her voice warm with concern, Dorothy said only, "Then how will you get to school?"

"My dad," he answered quickly. "My dad will take me."

And to his enormous relief—and instant despair—she nodded. "Okay," she said. "If you're sure." And she *whoosh*ed the door shut again. Jonathan stood perfectly still at the edge of the empty road as the bus rattled off, leaving him alone.

His breath came in short gasps. He was skipping school. He'd never done anything like this in his life. He flapped a hand at the diesel exhaust that hung in the air and turned toward the zoo entrance.

He needed to talk to his father. He had to make sure Dad knew that someone from Fish and Game was at the gate. And the TV reporter, too. A gun and a camera. Dad had to be told.

He had wanted something done about Trouble, to have him go away and never come back, and now they were going to kill him . . . and show the killing in the middle of everybody's dinner tonight. That wasn't what he'd asked for, was it?

*

The voices woke Trouble. They moved toward him, floating on the cool morning air. First he looked toward the enclosure that held Jake, but the older bear was still nowhere in view. Then he rose on his hind legs, trying unsuccessfully to peer through the dense trees that grew on each side of the zoo path. He dropped to all fours again. Where should he go?

He could smell as well as hear the humans, even if he couldn't see them. Although everything in this place was permeated with the smell of humans, he could make out distinctly the fresh scent of the ones moving toward him. The smell didn't put him on edge as much as it had just a few days earlier. He had grown almost accustomed to the way it clung to everything in this new territory, and accustomed, too, to the manner in which the disturbing smell seemed to be connected with food.

Soft food, easy to chew, to swallow.

Still, he wasn't so accustomed that he was going to stay here and wait for the humans to arrive. He'd go back instead to the place where he had dug in. He was all the way inside the zoo this time, inside both fences, but he had left a tunnel behind. He could still slip out easily enough.

And then . . . there they were! He could see them. Three tall humans, walking on their hind legs the way humans did. Coming toward him.

Trouble lumbered off the path and into the woods.

12

Go, Trouble!

JONATHAN made a wide circle around the television reporter and the Fish and Game ranger and arrived at the locked gate. Fortunately, Frank was in the gatehouse, getting set up for the day. The smell of popcorn already filled the air.

"Frank, I've got to see my dad. Do you know where he is?"

"Back by Jake's pen. They radioed me to say they'd found that wild brownie sleeping there this morning."

So Trouble was here, just waiting for someone to use a gun on him.

"Would you let me in?" Jonathan grasped the bars of the tall metal gate. He wanted to shake them, but he resisted. "There's something I've got to tell my dad."

Frank looked skeptical. "I don't know as how he'd want you in there with that bear loose and all."

"Please," Jonathan pleaded. "It's important. Really, really important. My dad would want me to tell him."

"Well . . . I don't know," Frank said, but even as he said it he opened the gate, just wide enough for Jonathan to slip through.

"Thanks!" Jonathan called, and he was off running toward the back of the zoo and Jake's pen before Frank could say another word.

He found his father and Pat Rawlings and Katie Doran, the education director, on the path in front of Jake's pen. Trouble was nowhere in sight.

"Jonathan!" his father exclaimed before Jonathan could catch his breath to begin to speak. "What are you doing here?"

"I had to tell you," Jonathan panted.

"They're out there." He bent over, his hands on his knees. "Outside the zoo. At the front gate."

"Who's out there?" The question was clipped, angry.

"The Fish and Game guy."

His father groaned. So did Pat and Katie.

"And somebody from the TV station, too."

His father cast a glance at the other two. Jonathan saw that Pat was carrying a gun, and it looked very much like the one the man from the Fish and Game department had with him.

"Just what we need," his dad said, speaking to the other adults, not to him. But when he turned back, his attention was fully on Jonathan. A hand clamped on each of Jonathan's shoulders.

"You don't belong here, son," he said. "That brownie is here again. Just as we came up, he disappeared into the woods. Right here." He waved an arm to indicate the large stand of trees just behind Jonathan. "And we're trying to catch up with him. So go!" He released his hold on Jonathan's shoulders and gave him a slight but definite push.

Jonathan held his ground. "What will you do when you catch him?" He knew the situation was urgent, that the slightest delay would make his father angry, but he had to ask.

"Never mind about that." Dad waved his hand again in the direction he wanted Jonathan to take. "Just get out of here before you miss your bus. I don't want to see you again until the day is over."

Jonathan didn't move. "Are you going to kill him?" he demanded. "Just like the Fish and Game guy out there, are you going to shoot him dead?"

His father looked surprised. For an instant, Jonathan thought Dad was going to remind him that last night he'd said he wanted Trouble killed. But his father didn't say anything about that. Probably only because any discussion would take too much time.

He merely shook his head. "No . . . no. We're not going to kill him. We'll dart him, put him to sleep. That is, if we can keep him from leaving the zoo. If he gets out the front gate or back out where he dug in, the ranger will have to kill him. Now, get out of here. I told you, you don't belong here. It's too dangerous!"

Strangely relieved, Jonathan turned and took off running.

He didn't go back to the bus stop, though. There was no point in that. His father hadn't checked the time, didn't realize he'd already missed the bus. As soon as the curving path had taken him out of his father's view, he stopped.

The three adults were going to walk this path—and probably the one on the other side of the stand of trees that Trouble had disappeared into—trying to herd the bear before them. But if they succeeded in getting Trouble to move, he might very well keep going until he ran out the front gate—to face the ranger's gun!—before anyone on the inside could stop him.

For an instant, Jonathan could feel Trouble's terror make his own muscles go limp, could feel the great heart slamming against his own ribs. Trouble hadn't meant to kill Mama Goose. A bear didn't understand killing. He understood noisy and quiet. He understood hungry and full. He understood lonely.

Trouble had to be lonely. Why else was he using up so much energy digging into the zoo just to be near Jake?

And now his loneliness was going to get him killed!

But he, Jonathan, could help. Even if his father thought he couldn't. He could stay right here and head Trouble back toward the adults and their tranquilizer gun. The bear hadn't touched him the night they had met nose to nose on the deck. Surely he wouldn't hurt him now.

Checking to make sure none of the adults

had come far enough along the path to be able to see him, Jonathan stepped over the low wooden fence at the edge of the path and darted into the shadow of the trees. Once there, he stopped to take a deep breath and to look around carefully. There was a brownie in these woods, and he could be anywhere!

Jonathan knew about bear attacks. Brownies are often more aggressive than black bears, but very few of them will attack a human. All they want to do is to get out of the way. But even if it's only one bear out of ten that will—or one out of a hundred—your luck runs out when you meet up with the bear that attacks you. And Trouble was going to be scared and running, for sure. He could react to anything in his path the way he'd reacted to Mama Goose.

What was it they told you to do if a brown bear attacked you? Play dead. That was it. Fight a black bear, play dead with a brownie. Cover the back of your neck with your hands, pull your knees up to protect your belly, and just lie there and hope the bear will go away.

A shiver rattled through his body, but Jonathan ignored it and moved deeper into the trees. Just as the adults couldn't see Trouble, because the stand of trees was so dense, they wouldn't be able to see him, either. And Trouble had to be lurking in here somewhere.

Jonathan's senses were strung so taut that he felt as though he might explode. And it was in that state of hyper-awareness that he stepped around a large bush and found himself face to face with the brown bear.

For an instant he couldn't breathe. He wondered if Trouble might be having difficulty breathing, too. The animal just stared with those small dark eyes, and neither of them made a sound. Beyond the trees, from the path Jonathan could no longer see, he could hear the adults. They were walking, calling to one another, coming closer. Trouble heard them, too. The brownie swung his great head this way and that, apparently looking for a way to escape.

Not this way! Jonathan thought. *You can't go this way!* And he began to jump up and down, waving his hands in front of Trouble's face, and shouting.

"Go!" he cried. "Go, Trouble! Get out of here!"

*

The young bear stood, rooted to the ground, amazed at the noise issuing from the boy. Humans were coming from behind, too. He could hear their footsteps and their voices. He could smell them. But directly in front of him was the smaller one he had seen before, the one he associated with the loaf of bread he had eaten, and noise was pouring out of his mouth.

Still, the voices coming from behind pushed at him! Trouble took another step toward the young one, but the boy held his ground. He kept yelling, kept flapping his arms up and down. Trouble stepped forward one more time, expecting the boy to give way. Still, the young one continued his infuriating dance.

For an instant, Trouble went completely still, caught, suspended. Then, trapped between the noise behind and the noise in front of him, he flattened his ears and popped his jaw in warning. Incredibly, the boy only yelled louder!

The confusion of humans on every side was too much. His grief and loneliness, his hunger and pain, were too much. And the human who bounced in front of him was no match for the power he knew resided in even a single swipe of his great paw. Trouble lifted one paw, ready to lunge, to strike.

The boy stopped jumping, stopped shouting, but still he didn't run away. He stood there and stared into Trouble's eyes. As though he thought himself the bigger bear!

The boy's stare unnerved Trouble, his bold stare combined with the voices moving up on him from behind. Trouble moaned, lifted his paw higher, moaned again. He was trapped, and all that stood between him and freedom seemed to be this scrap of a boy.

A noise came from the boy, this one soft, almost a whimper. And though he didn't know why he did it, the young bear lowered the paw he had intended to strike with, turned, and dodged away. He ran toward the ravine and the creek and the holes he had dug beneath the two fences that enclosed the zoo.

The bear had almost reached the first fence when he felt a sudden sharp sting in his shoulder. He twisted his head to snap at the thing that had penetrated his thick fur, his skin, his muscle. Snapped and missed. And then, strangely, after he had run a bit farther, his legs didn't seem to belong to him any longer. He stumbled and struggled to stay upright. A liquid warmth stole through his entire body.

As he went down, crashing into the brush at the base of the ravine, he found himself staring up at the boy, who had, incredibly, followed his flight. That was all he saw at the end, all he could remember . . . the boy.

13

A Lot Like Us

JONATHAN sat up in bed, listening. The neighbors surrounding the zoo would be complaining again. It had been almost a week since Trouble was captured, and he still banged around inside his enclosure, bellowing and moaning, day and night.

Was he, Jonathan, responsible for that, too—the fact that Trouble was miserable being confined, that the neighbors were being disturbed?

No. Not even his father would blame him for those things, though he had blamed him, it seemed, for everything else. The TV reporters being there. The Fish and Game people. But mostly Dad blamed Jonathan for being inside the zoo instead of on the school bus, for putting himself in danger to keep Trouble from rushing through the gate or back under the fence to be killed.

It didn't matter that everything had turned out all right. It didn't matter that Trouble hadn't had to be put down, that the television report had made the zoo personnel all look like heroes, that Jonathan hadn't been touched. Not so much as a nick from those long curving claws, those sharp teeth.

At first his father had been almost too angry to even notice that everything was okay. But then the relief had seeped in. Relief for Trouble, of course. His father truly didn't want to see the bear killed. But mostly relief that Jonathan hadn't been hurt. While the others went for a pallet to carry the drugged bear out of the ravine and into the den of the old polar bear exhibit where he could be held for a while, Dad had grabbed Jonathan, pulled him into the front of his denim jacket, and burst into rough tears.

"How could you?" he said, over and over again. "How . . . could . . . you? You might have been killed."

And even Jonathan knew what his father said was true. When he had stood, almost nose to nose with Trouble, when he had seen the desperation in the bear's eyes, he knew he had made the wrong choice. The young brownie might have swung at him as easily as he had at Mama Goose, and a boy would have about as much chance against such a blow as a too noisy goose. Everything had worked out, yes, but still he knew that he had made the wrong choice.

And how glad he was to be alive to know it.

Another roar from the captive Trouble reverberated through the neighborhood. Jonathan pulled the covers up to his chin, closed his eyes, and settled more deeply into his warm bed. Then slowly, silently, he let himself slip inside the bear. He let four strong legs carry him from one side of the concrete enclosure to the other, let Trouble's panic, his deep longing reverberate throughout his body.

"Animals," he was explaining to Rhonda just before he finally slept, "are a lot like us. They want, just like us."

*

Though Trouble's stomach was always full, the days he spent confined to the concrete room seemed to have no end. He had no knowledge of the negotiations that were going on, the reaching out to zoos all over the world, to find a new home for him. Nor would he have been impressed if anyone could have made him understand what these humans were doing. He wanted only what he had wanted since his mother sent him away: his old life back.

The day that one of the humans laid down a path of Fig Newtons, Trouble followed the path out of the concrete room, slurping one cookie after another without noticing where they led. An interesting new taste. He approved.

What he did not approve of was the small cage he found himself confined to after the last Fig Newton had disappeared. But he soon became sleepy—the cookies had been laced with Valium—and he was snoring mightily when the wooden crate was loaded into the belly of a passenger jet.

He slept so soundly, in fact, that he didn't catch a whiff of the 40,000 pounds of fresh salmon that had been loaded into the hold of the plane with him. The delicious aroma didn't even penetrate his consciousness . . . yet. When the Valium finally wore off and the young bear woke, he was many thousands of feet up in the air, somewhere over Canada. And then, of course, he smelled the salmon.

When the familiar and delicious aroma reached his nose, he proceeded to bang, to thump, to rattle his cage. He moaned and roared. And he made such a commotion that the pilot had no choice but to come on the intercom with an explanation.

"Ladies and gentlemen," he began, "don't worry about the noise you hear. You see, we have a very special passenger on board for this flight. And by the way, his name is Trouble!"

14

Home

JONATHAN taped the last box and carried it out to the trailer they would pull back to Anchorage.

"Can we go now?" he asked.

"To the zoo?" His mother smiled. It was a tired smile. They had been packing and loading for two days, but it was, nonetheless, a smile. "Sure," she said. "Our last official act before leaving Duluth will be a walk through the zoo."

Jonathan and his father had flown back to Duluth to help Mom and Rhonda pack. Now they would all drive to Anchorage. But first— Jonathan did a little jig right there on the sidewalk—they were going to visit Trouble!

How thrilled Jonathan had been when his dad had told him that the Lake Superior Zoo would take Trouble. The Duluth zoo even had a celebration when the bear arrived, complete with a band playing "Ya Got Trouble" from *The Music Man*. Jonathan wished they had been back in time to see it.

Dad said that when the veterinarian tranquilized Trouble to give him a thorough check, she'd discovered his broken jaw. That was probably the reason, she said, he'd been searching in town for food in the first place. The jaw was healing, and she'd pulled a couple of misaligned teeth. With that taken care of, Trouble could eat—with gusto—everything the zookeepers fed him. Apples, carrots, potatoes, meat, fish . . . all of it.

And now, at last, Jonathan would see Trouble in his new home.

"I guess we're ready," Dad said, and they all piled into the car and headed for the zoo.

When they arrived, Dad settled Rhonda

into her chair, and Jonathan took charge of pushing. She loved having him push, because he ran with her when she asked him to, something their parents rarely did.

"All set?" he asked.

"All set!" she replied. And they took off, parents trailing far behind.

They came around a corner and through a cement tunnel and screeched to a halt in front of the bear display. And there he was, in all his brown furry glory. Trouble!

"That's him?" Rhonda asked.

"Yep," Jonathan said. "That's Trouble!"

"He looks so . . ." She stopped and studied the brown bear. He was busy dismembering and eating an orange and didn't look up.

"Happy?" Jonathan filled in for her.

"Yeah," she said. "Like he *likes* being a zoo bear!"

Jonathan studied the brownie, too. Trouble had finished the orange and was now concentrating on some bread slathered with peanut butter. He did look like any properly zoo-bred bear. As though this were the life he had always lived. Or maybe the one he'd been looking for.

"Hi, Trouble," Jonathan said, tapping the glass that separated them from the large area where the bear was displayed. "How you doing, pal?"

Trouble sat back on his haunches and looked at his visitors for the first time. He licked peanut butter off his nose, then ambled over to the window. Putting a paw on the glass that separated them, he peered, first at Rhonda, then at Jonathan.

Jonathan put his hand on the other side of the window to meet the paw, and he closed his eyes. He was inside the bear, inside Trouble.

He could taste peanut butter on his tongue, feel his satisfied belly.

"He's looking at us," Jonathan whispered, looking down at Rhonda. "And you know what he's thinking?"

"What?" Rhonda asked. Her eyes were

shining, as they always did when he started the game.

"*Home,*" Jonathan said. "Trouble is thinking, '*At last, I'm home!*' "

Rhonda grinned and reached for her brother's free hand. "And we're going home, too, aren't we, Jonathan?"

"Yep," he said, turning back to watch their parents' slow approach. They looked happy to be together again, too. "The whole family. We're going home!"

*

Trouble watched the humans as they moved away. Whether he recognized the boy and remembered him would be impossible to know, but something held his attention. Only after they were out of sight and their scent no longer wafted back to him did he return to the feast waiting for him in his spacious rock-and-water home.

But now something else prompted him to lift his head and pause. From back in the holding area unavailable to the zoo's visitors, an-

other bear's voice rumbled. Trouble had been aware of the other brownie's presence from the beginning. The keepers who brought him food, who moved him out into the open enclosure and back again into his snug den, those same keepers watched over that other bear, too. Trouble could hear her at night in the den next to his. He could smell every place she had been when he came out into the open display.

And so he waited, patiently, in the way of bears, for the time when they would meet— for the day when, at last, he would no longer be alone.

Epilogue

A Bear Named Trouble is based on the story of a real bear, now residing in the Lake Superior Zoo in Duluth, Minnesota. As a young brown bear in Anchorage, Alaska, he earned the name Trouble by repeatedly breaking into the Alaska Zoo.

No one can know for certain what prompted him to dig his way into the zoo. Part of the motivation may have been that his mother had, no doubt, sent him off on his own that spring. He was about three and a half, the right age for her to decide it was time for them to separate. Since he was entirely alone, the young bear probably had no siblings to share his new life, and clearly, he was lonely. Loneliness must have brought him to the zoo to visit Jake.

His jaw had been broken in some accident we can only guess at, so he was probably searching for easy food, too.

On one of his excursions, Trouble did kill Mama Goose, who was, indeed, a favorite of the children who visited the Alaska Zoo. He didn't eat her, only killed her, probably because she was doing what geese do best, making a great deal of noise.

When the zoo personnel captured him at last, a television reporter and a ranger from the Fish and Game department were waiting outside. If Trouble had managed to emerge from the zoo before the curator could dart him, he would have been killed as a nuisance bear.

It is true, too, that Trouble was taken to Minnesota in the hold of a passenger plane, a service donated by Northwest Airlines, and that 40,000 pounds of fresh salmon accompanied him on the journey.

And the young bear did, indeed, arrive at the Lake Superior Zoo in Duluth to a band playing "Ya Got Trouble."

It is unusual to bring mature animals from the wild into a zoo, but the Lake Superior Zoo took a chance on Trouble to keep him from being put down. In return, he has adapted very well to his life there. Sometimes he even taps on the glass to get visitors' attention.

The already resident female grizzly, named Phoebe, started off as something of a challenge for Trouble. The first time the two bears were put in the display area together she trounced him pretty thoroughly. They were then separated for a long time but now are back together. At this writing, Phoebe remains dominant, because she is still bigger, but the two have become easy with one another. Trouble, at last, has what he was searching for . . . a companion.

The one aspect of Trouble's story as it is told here that is completely fictional is Jonathan and his family. I wanted to follow Trouble's journey through a child's eyes, so I created a boy who dreams his way inside animals.

My special thanks to Katie Larson, education director at the Alaska Zoo, Pat Lampi, curator at the Alaska Zoo, and Mike Janis, director of the Lake Superior Zoo, for their generous help when I was gathering information for this book.

Discovering and writing Trouble's story has been a special privilege.